First published in Great Britain in 2020 by
Hungry Tomato Ltd
F1, Old Bakery Studios,
Malpas Road, Truro,
Cornwall, TR1 1QH, UK

A CIP catalogue record for this book is available
from the British Library

Beetle Books and Hungry Banana are
imprints of Hungry Tomato Ltd

US Edition (Beetle Books)
ISBN 978 1 913440 43 5
UK Edition (Hungry Banana)
ISBN 978 1 913077 27 3

Printed and bound in China

Discover more at
www.hungrytomato.com
www.mybeetlebooks.com

AMAZING ART
FOR CREATIVE KIDS

BY EMILY KINGTON

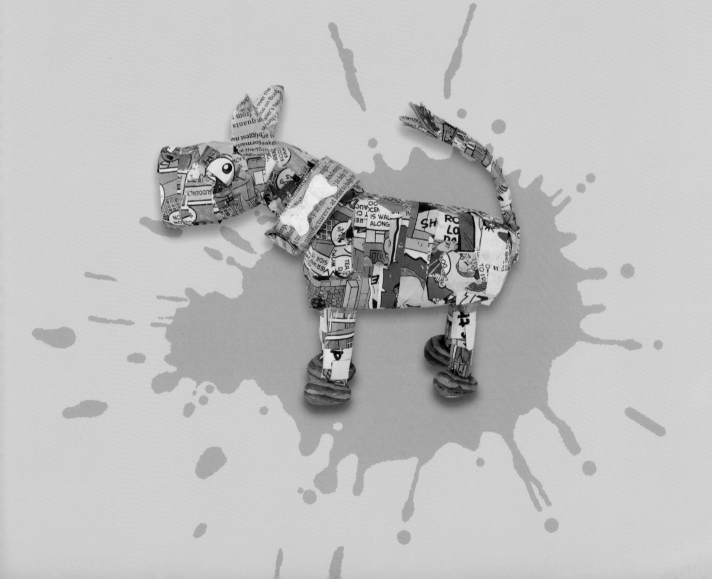

CONTENTS

MARVELOUS MODELS

INTRODUCTION

It's time to get creative! Pull out your paintbrushes and get ready to make some amazing, eye-catching art that will brighten up any room. Why not try some practical projects that not only look great, but will be really useful too? Or, get sculpting and make a whole bunch of crazy creatures and fun friends. There are no limits to what you could create! Just follow the simple step-by-step instructions and see where your inner artist takes you.

The following pages will help you get prepared by showing everything you will need for the projects in this book, along with some top tips and techniques to get you started. You'll also find a helpful page about supplies on page 92, at the back of the book.

TOP TIPS

1 For the paper-mache, prepare different sizes of newspaper/paper towel strips before you get sticky hands.

2 Protect surfaces from paint and glue. A plastic tablecloth is great but an old towel or a piece of cardboard will work well, too.

3 Clean paintbrushes between colors by using three small jars of water. Clean most of the paint off in the first, finish cleaning in the second, and store the brush in the third.

4 Give your models a final layer of school glue (PVA). It will dry clear and protect the surface.

5 Use scraps of cardboard to mix your paint and save on cleaning up!

MATERIALS

YOU WILL NEED

Masking tape to shape and attach different parts of the models together.

Pipe cleaners—12-inch (30cm) pipe cleaners are good.

Paper towels or tissue paper for a smooth final paper-mache layer and for padding out and shaping models.

Newspaper for strong layers of paper-mache and construction.

Paper rolls for construction and making small body parts.

Cardboard, such as cereal boxes and corrugated cardboard, which are easy to cut.

Thick paper/card and the **backboard** from a notepad.

Rubber bands and binder clips to hold things in place while gluing and shaping.

Paper clay for smaller projects and fine detail. Making it is quite time-consuming and messy, so it is best to buy this from a craft store. It comes ready to use in a block, is easy to model and air-dries.

Paper clips or thin wire to make small accessories.

Paper-mache powder good for surfaces and decorative details. You can buy this very

fine powder at most craft stores and online. Just mix with water, into a paste and it simply air-dries, ready for painting.

Cotton material for monster mummy bandages; an old pillowcase would be ideal.

School glue (PVA) and **all-purpose glue.**

Comic book

Brown and white string

Stones and gravel

Paper cups

Shoebox and a **white box**

Hessian fabric (optional)

Christmas ornament balls (baubles)

Craft sticks

Plastic bottles

Plastic eyes

Plant pot

Magnets

Chalk

Corks

Twigs

Beads

Balloons

MACHE METHOD

Tear different sizes of paper strips before you start.

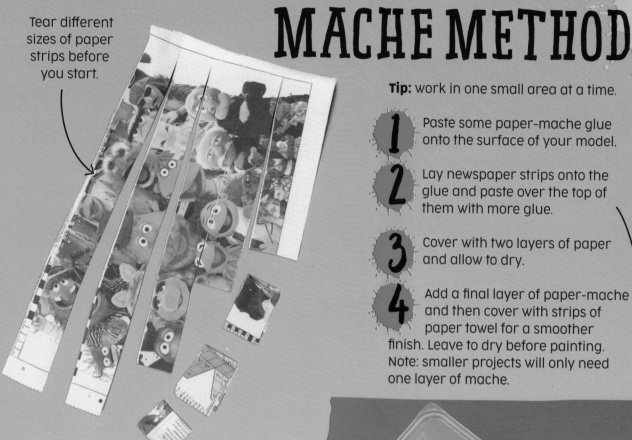

Tip: work in one small area at a time.

1 Paste some paper-mache glue onto the surface of your model.

2 Lay newspaper strips onto the glue and paste over the top of them with more glue.

3 Cover with two layers of paper and allow to dry.

4 Add a final layer of paper-mache and then cover with strips of paper towel for a smoother finish. Leave to dry before painting. Note: smaller projects will only need one layer of mache.

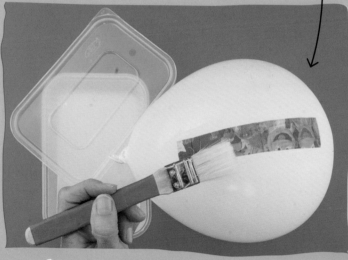

A GOOD RECIPE FOR PAPER-MACHE GLUE

This quantity is enough to complete a number of projects but you may have to mix the recipe twice for the larger projects. Keep leftover glue in an airtight plastic container and store in a cool place. Stir well before using again.

One cup of all-purpose flour

One and a half cups of water

Half a tablespoon of salt (add in humid climates to prevent mold)

One cup of school glue (PVA)

One tablespoon of cornstarch

1 Measure out the above ingredients into a plastic bowl or container.

2 Mix together well and store in an airtight container.

MODERN RECYCLED ART

Brighten up your room with modern art... this is just pure artistic indulgence and you can go totally wild!

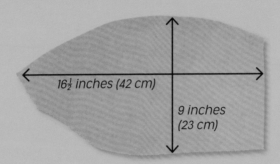

1 Cut out your mask face from stiff card.

16½ inches (42 cm)

9 inches (23 cm)

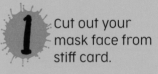

YOU WILL NEED

Stiff cardboard

Scraps of wood from your yard or park

Glue

Corks

Screws, beads, washers, buttons

Paper-mache powder

Florists' foam block, brown paper, wooden skewers and tape (to make a free-standing mask)

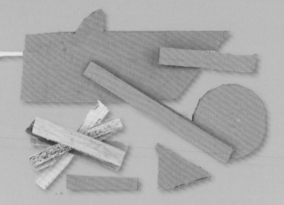

2 Cut out two sets of different shapes and find some small pieces of wood.

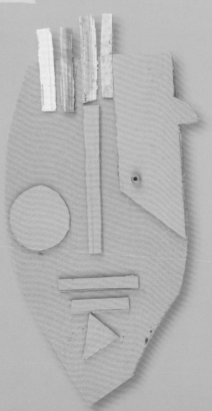

3 Arrange the shapes onto the face and glue them onto the surface.

4 Make your own stamps by sticking the beads, buttons or washers to the corks; here are a few examples.

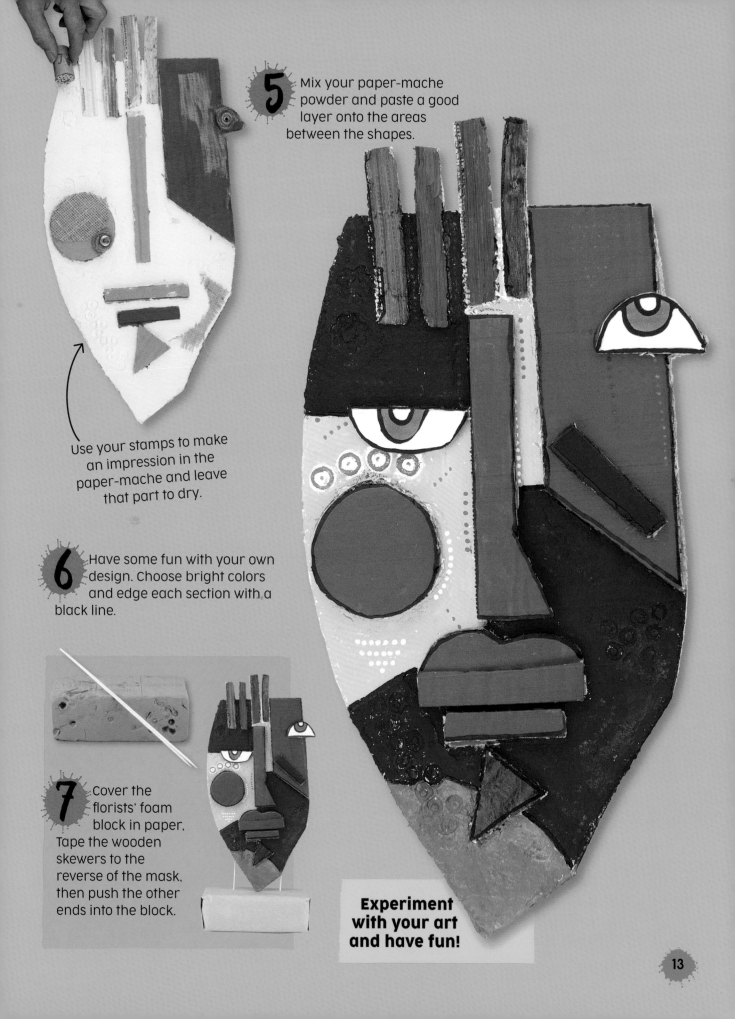

5 Mix your paper-mache powder and paste a good layer onto the areas between the shapes.

Use your stamps to make an impression in the paper-mache and leave that part to dry.

6 Have some fun with your own design. Choose bright colors and edge each section with a black line.

7 Cover the florists' foam block in paper, Tape the wooden skewers to the reverse of the mask, then push the other ends into the block.

Experiment with your art and have fun!

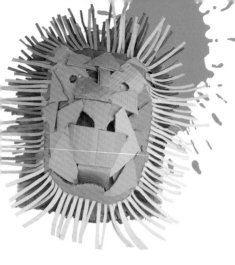

LION IN CARDBOARD

This lion wall mask has a bit of a WOW factor. You can almost hear it roar! This is like a 3D jigsaw puzzle and it can be any size you like...

YOU WILL NEED

Thin cardboard
Thick card
Hessian fabric (optional)
Paper
Glue
Newspaper
Masking tape
Thicker cardboard shapes

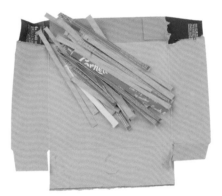

1 Cut some of the thin cardboard into narrow strips and set aside.

2 Cut a square base out of thick card. If you like, cover it in the hessian fabric so it overlaps the edges.

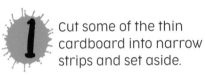

3 Draw a template for the lion's face on paper. Cut it out and glue it to the base.

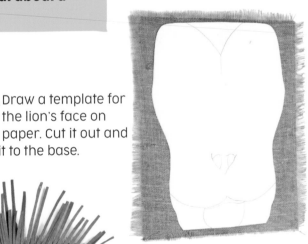

4 Glue some of the narrow cardboard strips to the outside of the template to form a mane.

5 Now pad out the facial area with scrunched-up newspaper. Use glue to keep it in place.

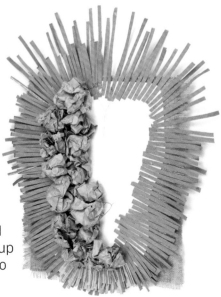

6 Use masking tape to start to shape the forehead.

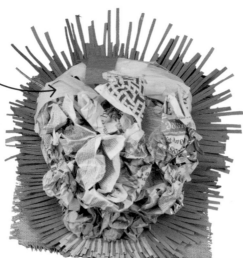

Cut shapes like these out of thicker cardboard and set aside.

7 Cut some of the thin cardboard into wider strips. Glue these strips to the base and bend them into the middle as shown. Glue to the scrunched-up paper below, using masking tape to help.

Construct the mouth and add the eye details by cutting holes in the cardboard.

Add a final layer of thin strips to the mane.

8 Glue some of the thicker cardboard shapes over the top to construct the nose, mouth, and chin areas. The nose needs to be raised and gaps left for the eyes and nostrils.

Nose

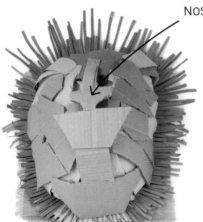

This king of the jungle makes a really striking piece of art!

LAZY FROG

Everyone loves a cheeky frog. This one is chilling on a lily pad in a nice cool pond.

YOU WILL NEED

Oval stone
Round stone
Gravel/stones
Stiff card/cardboard
Paint
Paper clay
Thick paper
Pipe cleaner and string
Glue

1 Once you have found suitably shaped stones, wash and dry them thoroughly. The round stone will be the body and the oval stone will be the head.

2 Cut out a circle from the cardboard large enough to accommodate Lazy Frog. This will be the pond. Paint it blue and leave to dry.

Make some round balls out of paper clay for the eyes.

3 Make a lily pad out of thick paper and paint it green. Draw on the leaf veins in pencil.

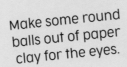

4 Paint your stones a bright lime green. Then, draw the mouth and nose onto the head.
Wind string around a pipe cleaner to make some legs and arms. Note that the arms are thinner and shorter than the legs.

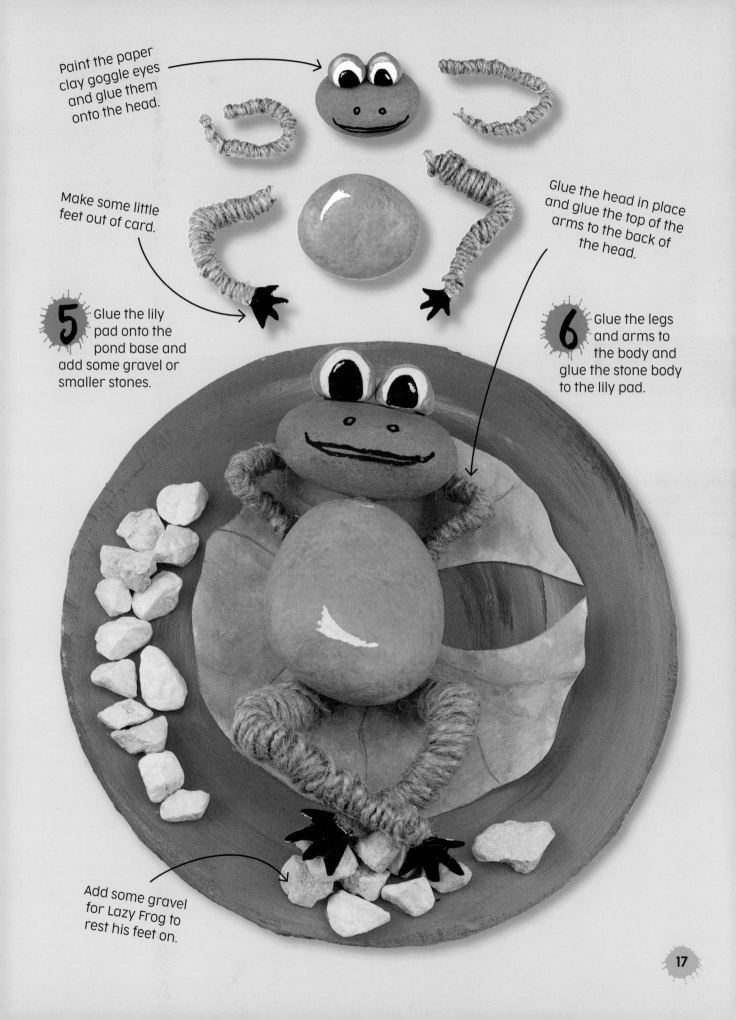

Paint the paper clay goggle eyes and glue them onto the head.

Make some little feet out of card.

Glue the head in place and glue the top of the arms to the back of the head.

5 Glue the lily pad onto the pond base and add some gravel or smaller stones.

6 Glue the legs and arms to the body and glue the stone body to the lily pad.

Add some gravel for Lazy Frog to rest his feet on.

ZEBRA MASH-UP

Different kinds of animals often befriend each other. Here is an mixed-up picture for your gallery. It may trick the viewer into thinking that what they are seeing is perfectly correct!

YOU WILL NEED

Thick paper or card

Small pieces of flat wood or thick cardboard

1 stiff piece of board (from the back of a notepad or similar)

Paint or coloring pens

Craft sticks

Glue

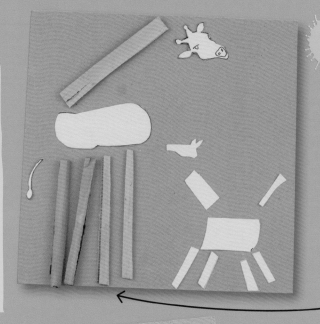

1 Cut out all of the white shapes you see here in thick paper or card. Then cut out the other shapes in thick cardboard, or trim small pieces of wood to size.

Strips of balsa wood or the dry bamboo used in potpourri would work well.

2 Make sure your giraffe will fit on your board, allowing space for the frame. Paint, or color in, the giraffe pieces to look like a **zebra,** and the zebra pieces to look like a **giraffe.**

3 Glue on the craft sticks in layers to make a frame around the edge of the board.

4 Position the giraffe in place and glue to the board, starting with the legs. Position the zebra in the pose shown and glue into place.

See how many people fall for the illusion. You may be very surprised!

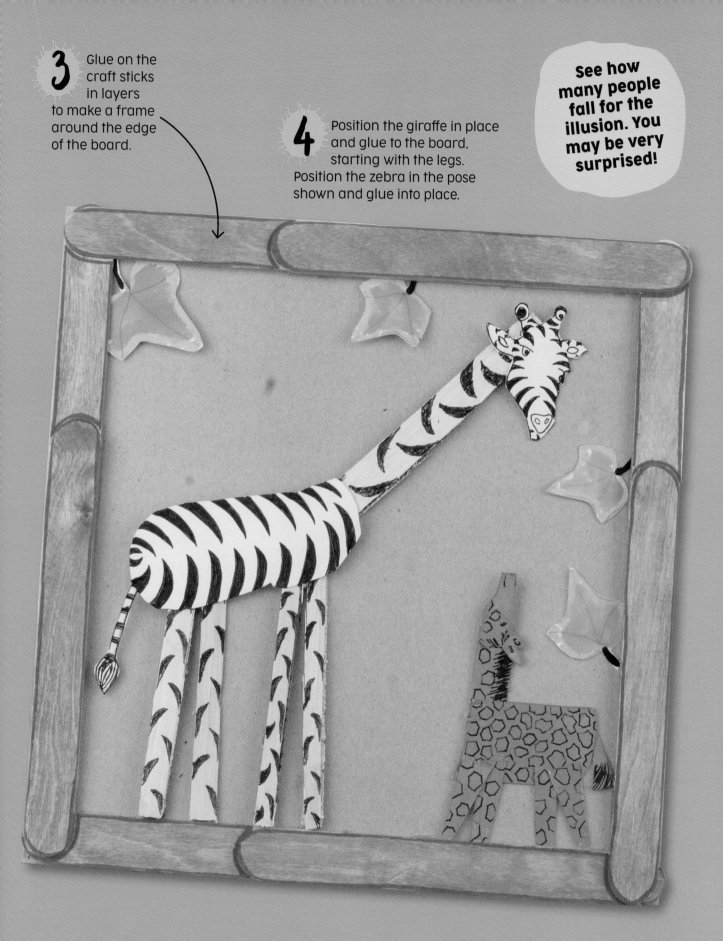

GARGOYLE DOOR HANGER

Here is a great way to keep trespassers out of your room: a super scary doorhanger.

YOU WILL NEED

1 sheet of paper
Cereal box
Thick cardboard
School glue
Craft sticks (optional: you can use plain card)
Masking tape
Paper clip
Paper-mache glue and paper towels (see page 11)
Tissue or paper-mache powder
Paint
String or ribbon

1 Make a paper template for the gargoyle.

2 Draw around the paper template onto your cereal box twice. Cut out two faces, and also a rectangular message board.

3 Use thick cardboard for the eyes, nose, and mouth. Cut out the shapes and glue them onto one of the faces. Then glue the craft sticks onto the reverse and, finally, glue the second cardboard face on the back, like a sandwich.

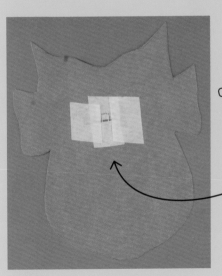

On the reverse of the other face, attach a paper clip with masking tape.

Glue on the message board.

4 Cover the face and board in two layers of paper-mache, avoiding the paper clip. Build up the facial features using tissues soaked in mache glue or use paper-mache powder (see pages 10–11). Leave to dry before painting.

5 Paint your scary gargoyle and leave it to dry. Then thread the string or ribbon through the paper clip, stick on a "Keep Out, Gargoyles Only" message and hang it from your bedroom door!

KEEP OUT! GARGOYLES ONLY!

CARDBOARD CITY

YOU WILL NEED

Cardboard boxes

Corrugated cardboard (often used in packaging)

Packing paper

Corks

Glue

Small twigs

1 Gather all sorts of different types of cardboard and boxes. Stores and supermarkets are a good source.

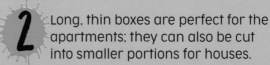

Don't throw anything away—even small pieces of cardboard can be really useful.

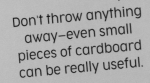

2 Long, thin boxes are perfect for the apartments; they can also be cut into smaller portions for houses.

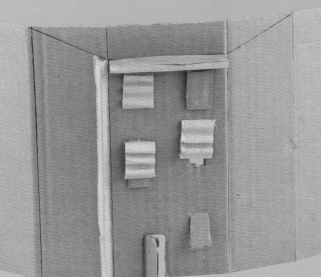

3 Cardboard is easy to bend into shape.

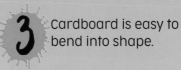

4 To make a house from cardboard you will need to measure out five sections as shown.

Make different sizes: short, tall, wide, and thin.

5 To make a sloping roof, measure ¾ inch (2 cm) down from the top of the front section and draw a line on both sides as shown. Then, cut out along the line.

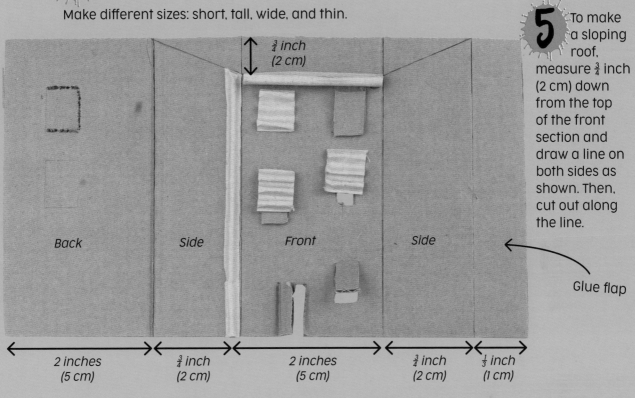

¾ inch (2 cm)

Back

Side

Front

Side

Glue flap

2 inches (5 cm)

¾ inch (2 cm)

2 inches (5 cm)

¾ inch (2 cm)

⅓ inch (1 cm)

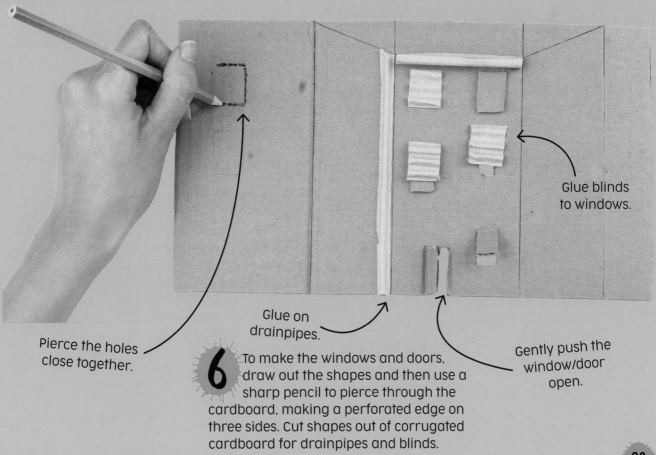

Pierce the holes close together.

Glue on drainpipes.

Glue blinds to windows.

Gently push the window/door open.

6 To make the windows and doors, draw out the shapes and then use a sharp pencil to pierce through the cardboard, making a perforated edge on three sides. Cut shapes out of corrugated cardboard for drainpipes and blinds.

23

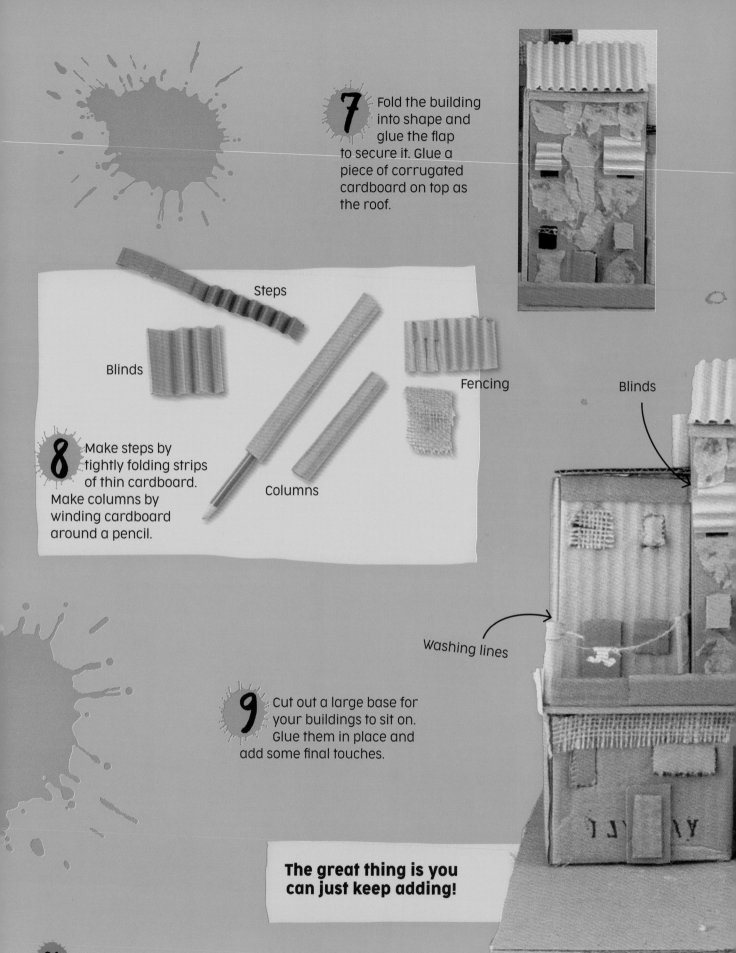

7 Fold the building into shape and glue the flap to secure it. Glue a piece of corrugated cardboard on top as the roof.

Steps

Blinds

Fencing

Columns

8 Make steps by tightly folding strips of thin cardboard. Make columns by winding cardboard around a pencil.

Blinds

Washing lines

9 Cut out a large base for your buildings to sit on. Glue them in place and add some final touches.

The great thing is you can just keep adding!

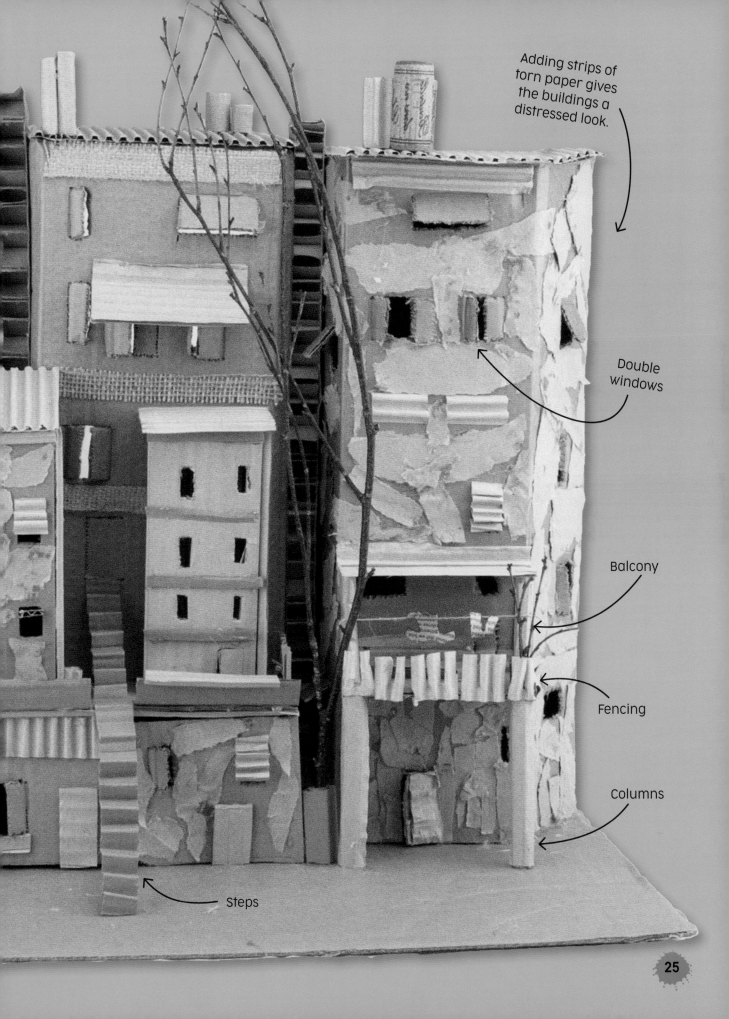

Adding strips of torn paper gives the buildings a distressed look.

Double windows

Balcony

Fencing

Columns

Steps

3D BABY ELEPHANT

Everyone loves baby elephants, and they make great subjects for artistic projects. Find a box and make your baby elephant fit it!

YOU WILL NEED

1 white cardboard box
Thick paper or card
Paper
Thick cardboard
Paint
Newspaper/magazine
Twigs
Glue
Black pen
Chalk

1 If you don't have a white box, don't worry—any box will do, and you can always paint it white.

2 Measure the inside of your box and cut out a piece of thick paper or card that will fit into the back of it. You will use this to mount your picture on.

3 Draw these shapes on a piece of paper and then cut them out. Use them as a template to draw the shapes onto thicker cardboard.

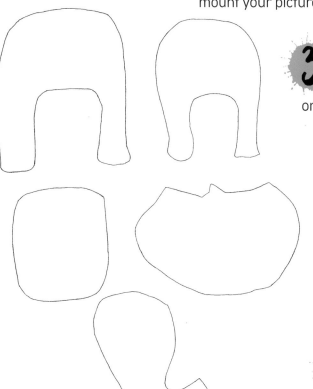

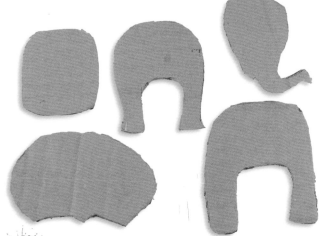

4 Once you are happy with their shape and size, cut out the shapes.

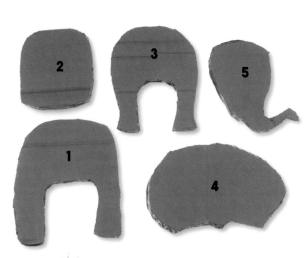

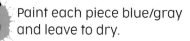

5 Paint each piece blue/gray and leave to dry.

6 Cut small leaf shapes out of color pictures in a magazine or newspaper. Glue them to the twigs.

7 On the piece of card you are using as your mount, arrange and glue on the background twigs and leaves.

Add detail to the painted pieces of the elephant with a fine-point black pen. Use chalk to highlight and give the elephant a dusty appearance.

Layer the elephant pieces in order from 1-5 (see step 5 for numbers). Glue each section into place.

8 Glue the mount into the back of the box. Add a larger twig in the foreground with different colored leaves.

"Baby elephant, chasing leaves" is ready to add to your gallery.

27

FUNKY CHICKEN BOOKENDS

This comic duo will be happy to keep your best books in order and will cheer up any boring old desk!

YOU WILL NEED

2 sturdy plastic bottles (approx. 7 inches/18 cm in height)

Gravel

Stiff cardboard
Glue

Cotton balls

Paper clay

Paper-mache glue and newspaper strips (see page 11)

Paint

1 Thoroughly clean your bottles and fill them with gravel to weigh them down.

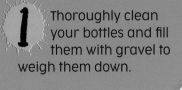

2 Cut out the shapes shown from the stiff cardboard. They should be big enough to reach the neck of the bottle.

3 Glue one piece of cardboard to each bottle. Glue cotton balls all over each bottle, but do not cover the cardboard.

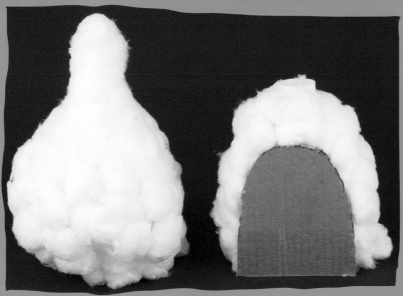

4 Give each chicken a nice round belly. Use a cotton wool ball for the head.

Eyes

Wattle (under the chin)

Beak

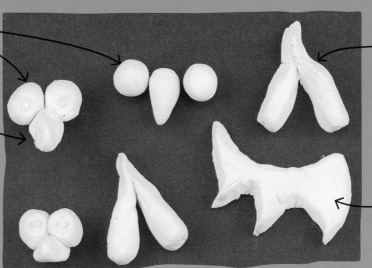

5 Make the chicken features out of paper clay. Once dry, paint them and set aside.

Comb (top of the head)

6 Cover each chicken in three layers of paper-mache (see page 11).

Stand the bottles on pots so you can reach underneath.

These happy hens make brilliant bookends!

7 Once the paper-mache is dry, paint the hens with your own design and glue on the features.

HUNGRY TOAD

If you want somewhere on your desk to store your pens, pencils, scissors, and other essential items, how about a great big, wide-mouthed toad to do the job?

YOU WILL NEED

Large take-out coffee cup or yogurt pot
Paint
Cardboard
Rubber band
Pipe cleaners
Cardboard tube
Masking tape
Glue
Paper clips
Tissue paper
Paper towels
Beads
Newspaper

1 Paint the inside of your clean coffee cup or yogurt pot any bright color.

2 Draw these shapes onto the cardboard and cut them out.

6½ inches (17 cm)

6 inches (15 cm)

6 inches (15 cm)

3 Position the larger shape underneath the cup and the smaller shape on top, and hold in place with a rubber band.

4 Place a pipe cleaner inside the cardboard tube and fix in place with masking tape.

Bend the tube to make a curve.

5 Glue the smaller feet to the ends of the pipe cleaner in the tube, then cut out smaller pieces of pipe cleaner and glue on as shown. Attach the larger feet to 2 more pipe cleaners using paper clips or glue. Wind the other end of the pipe cleaners around the elastic band.

Attach the middle of the kitchen roll to the back of the cup with masking tape as shown.

6 Now you will need to pad out the shape using tissue paper and **lots** of masking tape. Start at the head and work your way down to the back legs.

Wind folded pieces of paper towel around the legs until you get a nice, rounded, and well-covered toad!

Put a mound of tissue paper on top of his head to make a bump.

Use lots of tape. You can add more layers on top until you are happy.

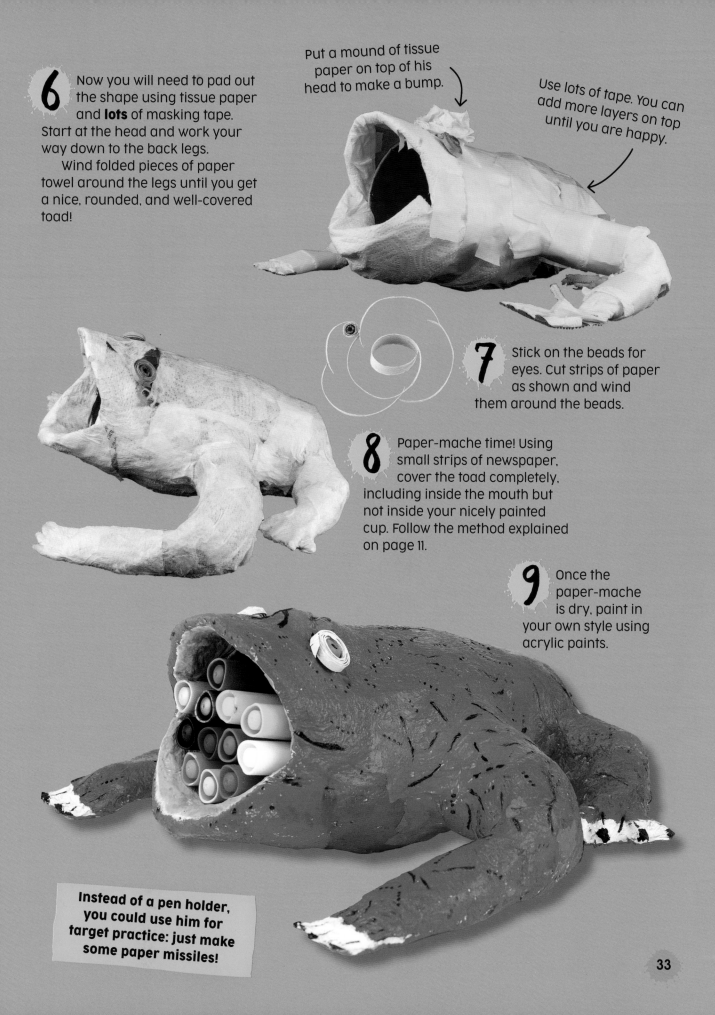

7 Stick on the beads for eyes. Cut strips of paper as shown and wind them around the beads.

8 Paper-mache time! Using small strips of newspaper, cover the toad completely, including inside the mouth but not inside your nicely painted cup. Follow the method explained on page 11.

9 Once the paper-mache is dry, paint in your own style using acrylic paints.

Instead of a pen holder, you could use him for target practice: just make some paper missiles!

BIRD BOX

How about this little bird box art supplies tidy? It's *cheep cheep*... and it will be great to keep everything you need for your art in one place!

YOU WILL NEED

5 Christmas ornament balls (various sizes)

Paper-mache glue and thin strips of newspaper (see page 11)

Paper clay

1 shoebox

Newspaper

Masking tape

School glue (PVA) and strong glue

Paint

Paper cups

1 Paper-mache each ornament with two layers of paper in one go and leave them to dry (see page 11).

2 Make the birds' eyes and beaks out of paper clay. Leave to dry before painting.

3 Remove the lid of the shoebox. Use it to make a centre partition for your bird box to a height of 3 inches (7.5 cm).

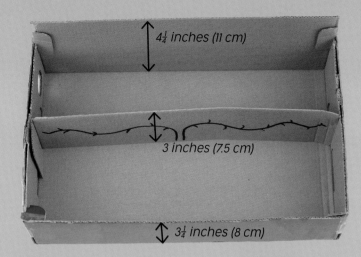

$4\frac{1}{4}$ inches (11 cm)

3 inches (7.5 cm)

$3\frac{1}{4}$ inches (8 cm)

4 Trim the shoe box on three sides to a depth of about $3\frac{1}{4}$ inches (8 cm), but leave the back panel deeper (about $4\frac{1}{4}$ inches/11 cm).

5 Draw some designs on the newspaper for the back panel, trim them to size, and glue them on.

6 Cover the outside of the box in newspaper. Finish the edges with masking tape to make it more robust. Draw your own design onto the outside, and paste on a layer of school glue (PVA) to protect the surface.

7 Paint your birds (the stump of the ornament should be at the bottom). Glue on the beaks and eyes with strong glue.

8 Decide how many paper cups you want to include and glue them into place. Glue the stump of each bird onto the box or cups using strong glue.

A place for everything— and everything in its place.

Arrange your box to suit your needs. See how tidy we artists can be!

MONSTER MAGNETS

These are great fun and can be given as presents—they won't take too much time to make.

YOU WILL NEED

Paper-mache powder
Card (a cereal box is perfect)
Round object (about 2 inches/5cm in diameter)
School glue (PVA)
String (optional)
Sharp pencil
Paint
Magnets

1 Prepare the paper-mache powder in advance (see page 10).

2 Draw five circles onto card using your round object as a template. Copy the Frankenstein's monster drawing by hand and cut out all of the shapes.

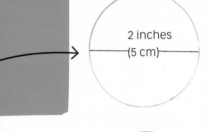

2 inches (5 cm)

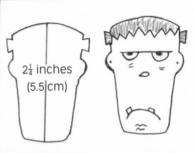

2¼ inches (5.5 cm)

3 If you are going to give your Monster Magnet scary string hair, glue the hair to the round disk first and allow the glue to dry.

4 Take a small blob of paper-mache mixture and pat it onto the round card, making a domed shape. Dip your finger in some water and smooth out the surface.

Use the nib of a sharp pencil to carve out details.

Carve out different shaped mouths.

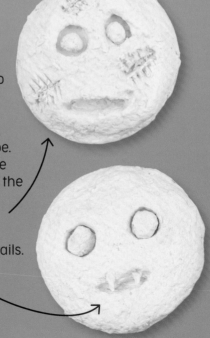

5 Carve out eye sockets, using the end of a pencil. Roll two equal amounts of mixture in the palm of your hands to make goggle eyes and pop them in the eye sockets, pressing down gently. Make sure you leave a bit of the socket showing so you can paint it a different color.

Score the paper-mache with a pencil to represent eyelashes or wrinkles.

Take tiny pieces of mixture, roll them in your palms, and flatten them to make spots.

6 Leave to dry before painting with bright colors, on both sides, and leave to dry.

You may find it easier to use a fine-point pen to to add small details.

For the Dracula magnet, draw the hairline with a pencil before painting it black.

Carve out the monster's features, hairline, eyes, and mouth, then add teeth!

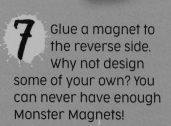

7 Glue a magnet to the reverse side. Why not design some of your own? You can never have enough Monster Magnets!

These magnets are great to keep treasured photographs on your fridge.

CHEEKY CHIMPANZEE

YOU WILL NEED

1 small, clean plant pot
Brown string
Glue
Stiff card
Small sponge
White string
2 beads
Pipe cleaners
Paint

This little chimpanzee would make an impressive gift for someone you know. But he is so cheeky you may not want to part with him!

1 Wind the brown string tightly around the plant pot from top to bottom. Use glue to attach the string to the pot on the first and last rows.

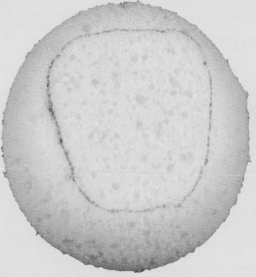

2 Draw the face shape on the card as shown and cut it out. Draw an outline of the face on your sponge, making it slightly bigger than the card face.

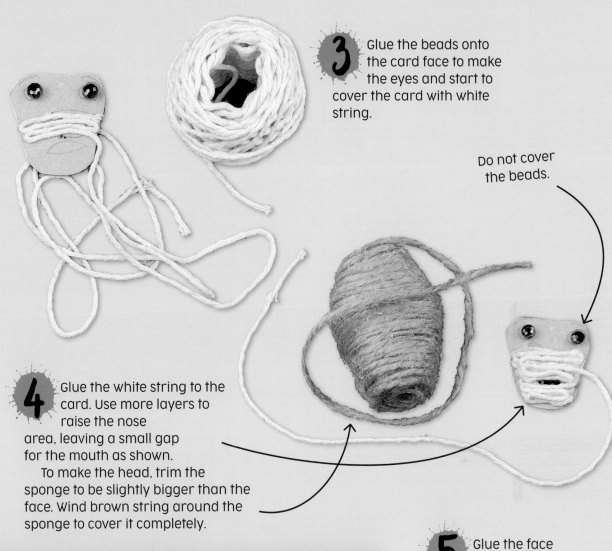

3 Glue the beads onto the card face to make the eyes and start to cover the card with white string.

Do not cover the beads.

4 Glue the white string to the card. Use more layers to raise the nose area, leaving a small gap for the mouth as shown.
To make the head, trim the sponge to be slightly bigger than the face. Wind brown string around the sponge to cover it completely.

5 Glue the face to the head.

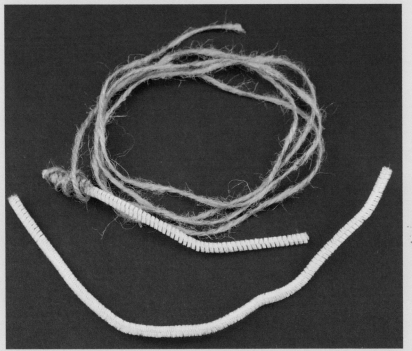

6 Measure out a length of pipe cleaner to make the arms. Wind two layers of brown string around it.

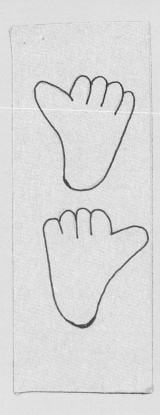

7 Draw some chimpanzee feet on the card and cut them out.

The legs need to be thicker than the arms.

8 Measure out another length of pipe cleaner for the legs. Glue the feet to each end, then wind layers of string around the pipe cleaner, using more than you used for the arms.

Use a marker pen to draw on the nose.

9 Glue the head, arms and legs to the pot.

Paint the feet before fixing to the pot.

Chimpanzee is ready to plant. What a great gift!

GREEDY GARBAGE MONSTER

Do you need something to throw all your trash in? Here is a great, easy-to-make monster that can collect all of your trash and keep it off the floor!

YOU WILL NEED

Small bucket or trash can for a template/mold (if you can't find one, don't worry—just pack a plastic bag full of newspaper to form the shape)

Cardboard

A large plastic bag (any plastic bag will do)

Paper-mache glue and thin strips of newspaper (see page 11)

Newspaper

Binder clip

Masking tape

Tissues

School glue (PVA)

Paper towels

Paint

1 For the feet and base, draw around the bottom of the trash can or bucket onto cardboard, creating a circle.
Hand-draw chunky monster feet on one side of the circle and cut out the shape.

Corrugated cardboard is easy to use, and nice and bendy

2 Measure out enough cardboard to wrap around the back of your trash can or bucket. Draw the shape shown and cut it out.

3 Place the plastic bag over the top of your bucket or trash can. Try and leave wrinkles and folds on one side, because this will form the monster's saggy belly.

Use newspaper paper-mache (see page 11) to cover the plastic bag, keeping the wrinkles and folds at the front.

4 Once covered, and before it's completely dry, carefully remove the trash can or bucket and pack out the inside with newspaper instead.

Turn over the top to form a lip, then use a binder clip at the front to form a 'V' shape.

Leave to dry overnight and then glue the base feet onto the bottom.

5 Attach the arms, face, and eyes using masking tape.

Add tissue and padding to the feet, eyes, hands and face.

For fuller lips, add thinly rolled newspaper using school glue and masking tape.

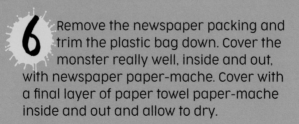

6 Remove the newspaper packing and trim the plastic bag down. Cover the monster really well, inside and out, with newspaper paper-mache. Cover with a final layer of paper towel paper-mache inside and out and allow to dry.

GREEDY GARBAGE MONSTER

What a great place to throw your trash!

These goggle eyes are sure to follow you around the room.

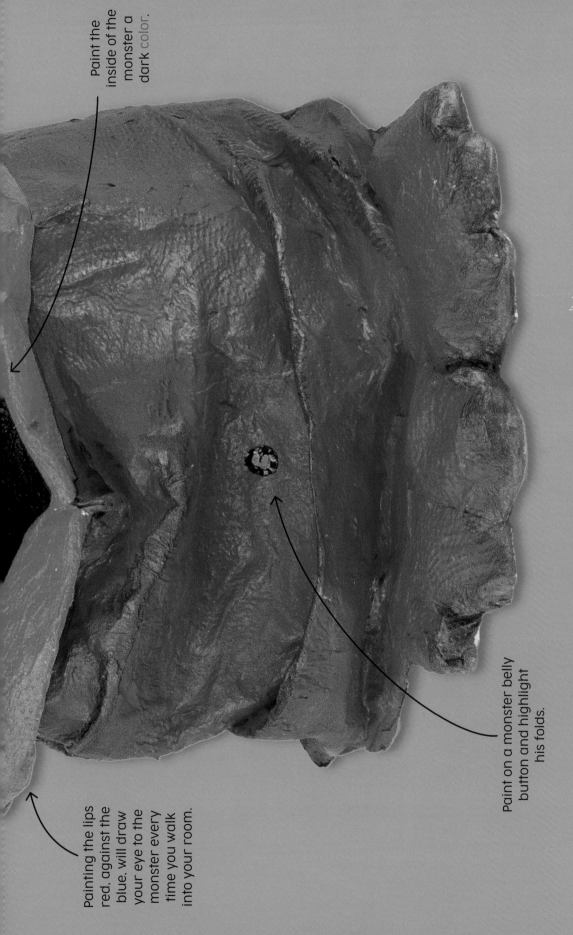

Paint the inside of the monster a dark color.

Painting the lips red, against the blue, will draw your eye to the monster every time you walk into your room.

Paint on a monster belly button and highlight his folds.

7 Paint your greedy garbage monster with acrylic paint. Once dry, he will need a good coat of school glue (PVA), both inside and out.

ORANGE & MELON PARTY BOWLS

Make these for your next party and fill them with delicious popcorn to share with your friends.

YOU WILL NEED

1 large and 1 small mixing bowl (for a template/mold)

Plastic bags x 2

Masking tape

Long newspaper strips and paper towels

Paper-mache glue (see page 11)

Paint

School Glue (PVA)

1 Cover the outside of each bowl with a plastic bag, using masking tape.

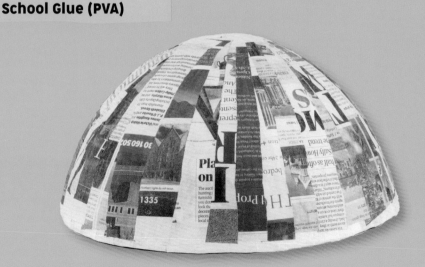

2 Cover the outside of the plastic with long strips of newspaper paper-mache (two successive layers in one go).

3 Leave until almost dry and then gently remove them from the molds. Press down on the base inside each bowl with your palm until they sit nicely.

Using small strips of masking tape, cover the rim of each bowl for a clean edge.

Paper-mache the larger bowl, inside and out, with two more layers; leave some of the masking tape showing at the top and leave to dry completely.

Repeat for the smaller bowl, but for the final layer, use textured paper towels for a pitted finish on the outside, like orange peel.

4 Mix your paints to get the most authentic colors. Paint the large bowl like a melon. Use a marker pen to paint pips inside the bowl.

5 Repeat for the small bowl, painting it to look like an orange. Leave both to dry before covering with two layers of school glue (PVA) for a waterproof coat!

SCARY SPIDER FAMILY PAPERWEIGHT

YOU WILL NEED

Paper
Large stone
Pipe cleaners
Paper clay
Paint
Sponge
Paper towel
School glue (PVA)

Do the papers on your desk keep falling on the floor or blowing away? This scary spider paperweight is a great way to keep your papers in one place.

1 Practice drawing a spiderweb on paper first, then try drawing it onto the stone in pencil to perfect your technique!

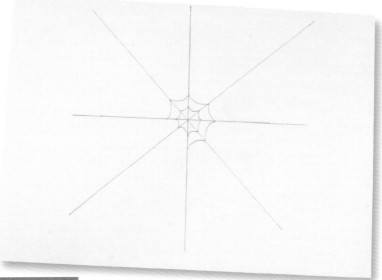

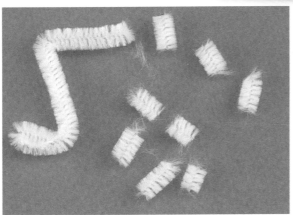

2 Use pipe cleaners to make eight legs and then cut another two pipe cleaners into small pieces.

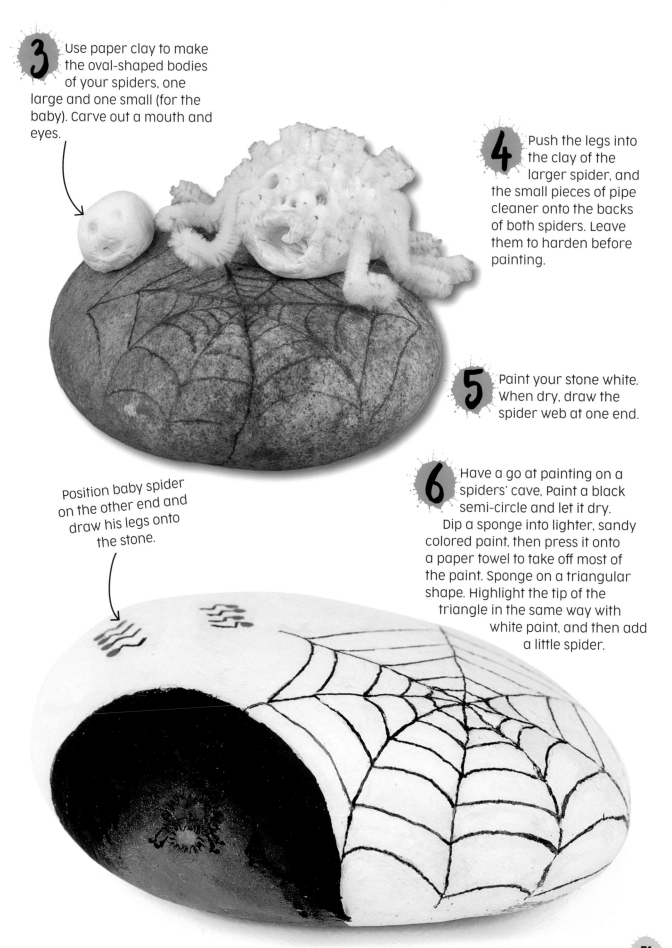

3 Use paper clay to make the oval-shaped bodies of your spiders, one large and one small (for the baby). Carve out a mouth and eyes.

4 Push the legs into the clay of the larger spider, and the small pieces of pipe cleaner onto the backs of both spiders. Leave them to harden before painting.

5 Paint your stone white. When dry, draw the spider web at one end.

Position baby spider on the other end and draw his legs onto the stone.

6 Have a go at painting on a spiders' cave, Paint a black semi-circle and let it dry. Dip a sponge into lighter, sandy colored paint, then press it onto a paper towel to take off most of the paint. Sponge on a triangular shape. Highlight the tip of the triangle in the same way with white paint, and then add a little spider.

7 Paint your spiders and glue them onto the stone, ready for desk duty!

Top tip: practice drawing on rough paper first for a perfect finish.

MONSTER COAT HANGER

Meet Frank! Imagine the surprise anyone will have opening your closet and finding Frankenstein's monster hanging from the rail, looking after your clothes!

YOU WILL NEED

Paper

Cardboard

Paper-mache glue and paper towels (page 11)

Paper-mache powder or tissue paper soaked in glue

Coat hanger

Strong tape

Pipe cleaners

School glue (PVA)

Paint

Sponge

String

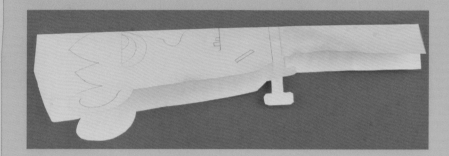

1 On folded paper, copy half the face along the fold, cut out for a symmetrical face template.

2 Draw around your template onto cardboard. Use a fine-point pen to draw scars, hairline, and features. Cover both sides in a thin layer of paper-mache, using paper towels (see page 11), and leave to dry.

You can see Frank's details through the paper-mache layer. Mix your paper-mache powder and use it to construct the eyes, nose, scars, teeth, and bolts.

3 When dry, tape the coat hanger to the reverse as shown, and cover with two layers of paper towel paper-mache to fix in place. Leave to dry before painting.

Do not cover the hook with paper-mache.

4 Make Frank some hands. To do this, draw around your own hands, on some cardboard. Cut them out and glue on the pipe cleaners as veins, then cover in paper-mache.

Once dry, give them the monster paint treatment!

Make a hole in the wrist, ready to thread the string through.

MONSTER COAT HANGER

To make this a great scary coat hanger – you need to finish him off by joining the hands and head together as shown below

Shade areas using a sponge. Dab the sponge on paper towel first to take off most of the paint.

5 First tie some string to each side of the hanger (make sure the string is longer than the sleeves). Then place the head and coat hanger in your garment. Thread the string down through the sleeves.

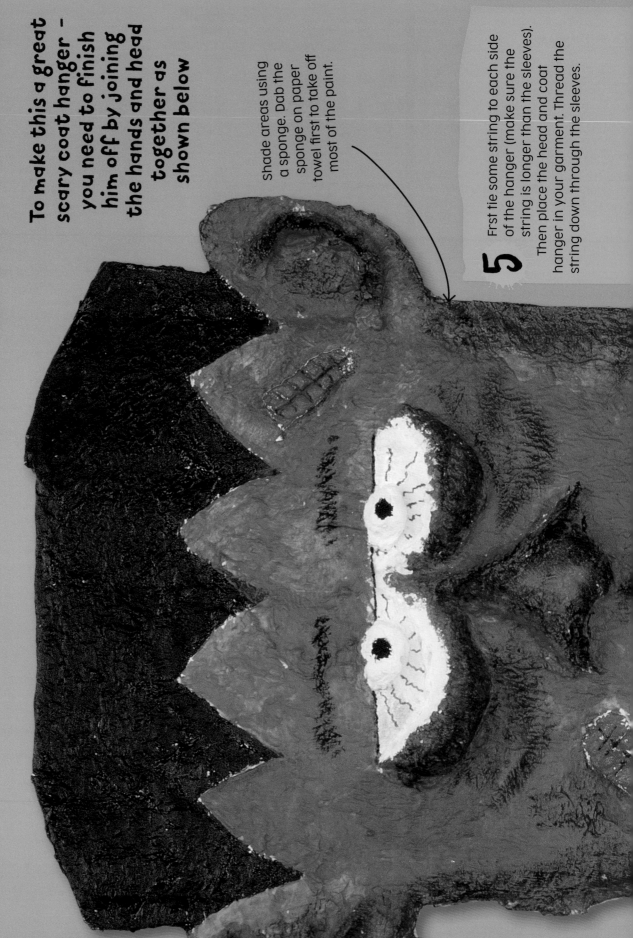

Now thread the string through the holes in the hands, making sure they are the correct length for the hands to show at the ends of the sleeves.

He is now ready to hang out in your room!

Give him a final coat of school glue (PVA) to make him good and strong.

COMIC STRIP DOG

It's amazing what you can make with a few cardboard tubes. This little dog is pretty cool and really stands out from the crowd.

YOU WILL NEED

3 cardboard tubes
Masking tape
Old comic book
Paper-mache glue
(page 11)
Newspaper
Paper clay
Glue

1 Squash one of the cardboard tubes flat and cut it into two pieces lengthwise. Use one portion to make the head and neck.

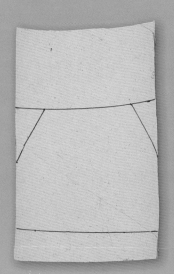

2 Draw the lines as shown and cut out the shape.

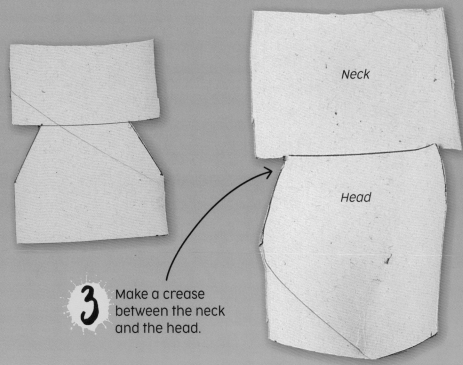

Neck

Head

3 Make a crease between the neck and the head.

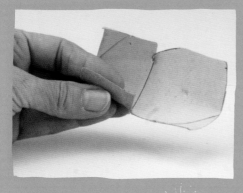

4 Curl the sides of the neck toward each other as shown. Make a crease to shape the dog's head. Bend the neck down toward the head and secure with masking tape.

5 Cut out the ears from the spare piece of card. Fold them as shown and attach with masking tape.

6 For the body, bend another cardboard tube as shown and seal one end with masking tape.

Attach the head to the body with tape.

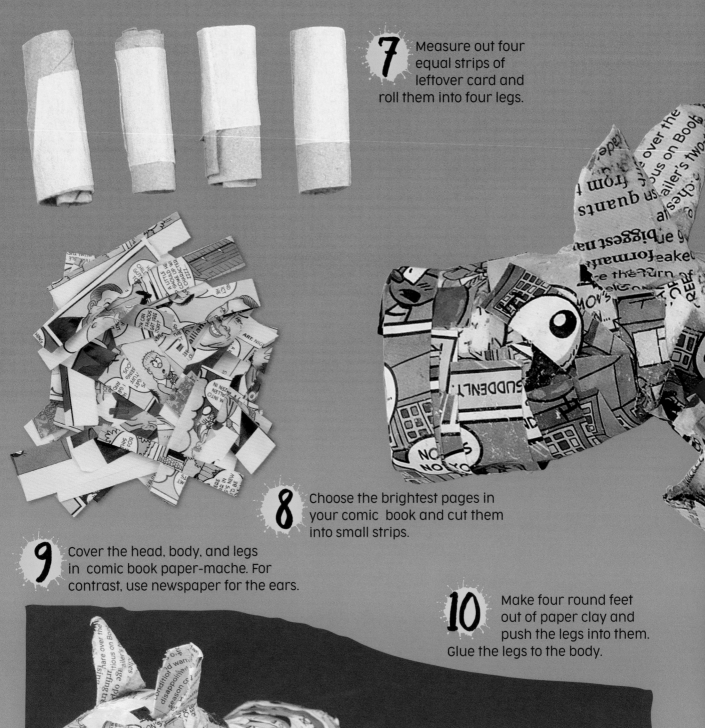

7 Measure out four equal strips of leftover card and roll them into four legs.

8 Choose the brightest pages in your comic book and cut them into small strips.

9 Cover the head, body, and legs in comic book paper-mache. For contrast, use newspaper for the ears.

10 Make four round feet out of paper clay and push the legs into them. Glue the legs to the body.

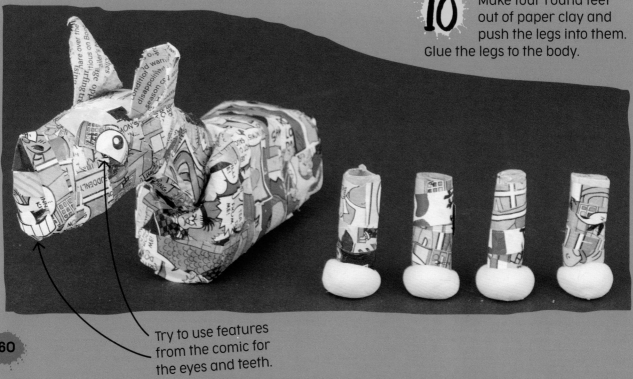

Try to use features from the comic for the eyes and teeth.

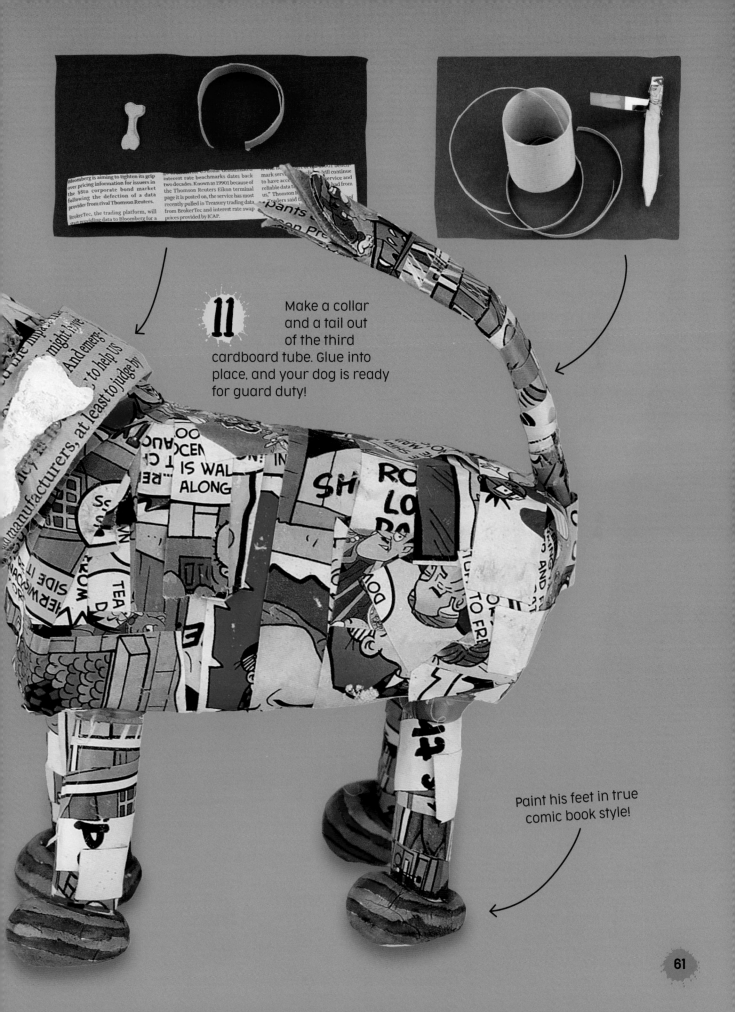

11 Make a collar and a tail out of the third cardboard tube. Glue into place, and your dog is ready for guard duty!

Paint his feet in true comic book style!

DINOSAUR MACHE

Have you ever wanted a friendly dinosaur to sit on your shelf? Here is an easy-to-make giant Brontosaurus!

1 Inflate the balloon, but do not fully inflate it. This will make it less likely to pop when masking tape is stuck on it.

2 Cut the cardboard tubes in half and stick them together with masking tape, as shown. Attach them to the bottom of the balloon.

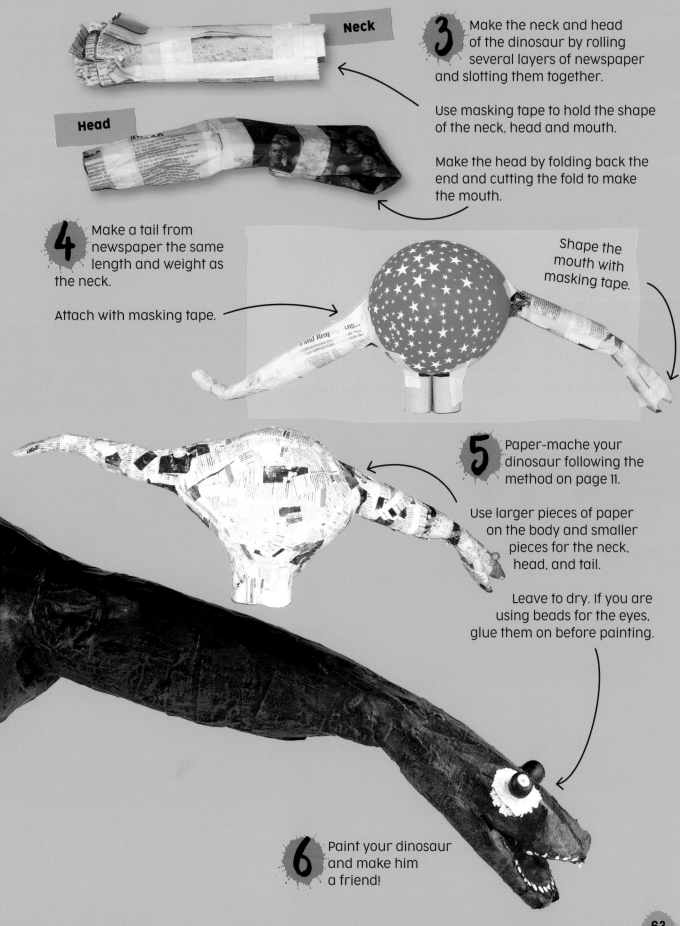

Neck

Head

3 Make the neck and head of the dinosaur by rolling several layers of newspaper and slotting them together.

Use masking tape to hold the shape of the neck, head and mouth.

Make the head by folding back the end and cutting the fold to make the mouth.

4 Make a tail from newspaper the same length and weight as the neck.

Attach with masking tape.

Shape the mouth with masking tape.

5 Paper-mache your dinosaur following the method on page 11.

Use larger pieces of paper on the body and smaller pieces for the neck, head, and tail.

Leave to dry. If you are using beads for the eyes, glue them on before painting.

6 Paint your dinosaur and make him a friend!

GONE FISHING

Tin cans are a brilliant resource for making all sorts of interesting art. Think outside the box and be creative.

YOU WILL NEED

Use materials you have readily available for added detail. You could use:

Cardboard

Large tinned food can

Two different types of string

Masking tape

Glue

Paint

Large and small soda cans

Stiff paper or thin card

Variety of beads, nuts, bolts, corks, washers, and a spring

Smaller food cans

Pipe cleaners

For the fishing rod:

Skewer, 2 soda-can tabs, 1 nut and string

THE FISHING BEAR

Clean your collection of cans thoroughly.

large food can

small soda can

Safety! Be careful of sharp edges on cans

small food can

1 Cut out the bear's head from stiff cardboard. Draw around the large tin and cut out a disk.

Measure and cut out a cardboard sleeve to wrap around the large tin.

2 Braid three lengths of string to make some legs for the bear. Knot the string together at the top, and use masking tape to hold in place while you braid.

Keep going until the braid is long enough for the legs. Add tape at both ends for the feet.

3 Glue the sleeve onto the tin and paint on some stripes.
Glue on the legs and disk as shown.

4 For his body, wind some string around a soda can. You only need to glue the first and last row to the can.
Cut out his arms and two fish from thin card, and glue them on.

Paint his face and add features, using beads, nuts, and bolts. Glue onto the body.

5 Make a fishing rod: glue the nut to the bottom of the skewer for the reel, glue one soda tab to the middle and one to the top. Thread the string through the two tabs, leaving a length hanging down for the line and finish by winding the string around the nut.

Glue the body to the base and glue the fishing rod onto the side.

THE CRAFTY CAT

Beady eyes

6 Cut out the cat's head from cardboard.
Wind string around the side and bottom of a small food can for the cat's body, and around a pipe cleaner for the tail.

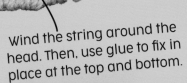

Wind the string around the head. Then, use glue to fix in place at the top and bottom.

7 You can dress up the cat using small, recycled household items.

Make a fish for crafty cat to eat.

Cut pieces of string for the whiskers.

8 Decorate the head and body with spots and stripes, and glue together.

TIN CAN DOG

9 Glue two soda-can tabs on the top of a small soda can for ears. Cover the can in brown string.

Find an old spring to make a tail.

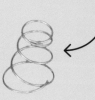

11 Wind string around two corks and paint the ends silver for his feet.

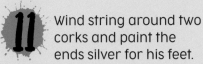

10 For the body, cover a soda can in white and brown string.

Paint on extra silver stripes.

13 Use small, recycled household items to make his eyes and tongue and glue his head onto the body.

Glue on the feet and add the spring for his tail.

12 Add some stripes, using brown string. Cover both ends of the soda can as shown and wind some brown string into a ball for the neck. Glue it onto the can.

Give them pride of place on your shelf!

BRILLIANT BUGS

Here is a motley collection of monster bugs. One can fly, one can hop, and the other is in disguise!

YOU WILL NEED

Cardboard tube
Masking tape
Newspaper
Cardboard
Pipe cleaners
Paper-mache glue (see page 11)
Small strips of newspaper
Paint
Small piece of plastic
Paper clips
School glue (PVA)
Paper towels
Plastic eyes (optional)
Thin twigs

HOPPING BUG

1 Fold the cardboard tube in half lengthwise. Secure both ends with masking tape and trim one end to shape the tail.

2 For the head, roll some sheets of newspaper, fold them over, and attach them with masking tape to the other end, as shown.

For the lower jaw, cut out a small strip of card and attach underneath the newspaper head.

Make two back legs.

Make four front legs.

3 Use a pipe cleaner to shape each of the larger back legs as shown, shaping the foot at one end and leaving a small portion at the other to tape the leg to the body.
Make the four smaller legs with the remaining pipe cleaners as shown. Wind masking tape around each of the pipe cleaners and attach to the body with masking tape.

4 Cover the body with a layer of newspaper paper-mache (see page 11). Leave to dry before painting.

Cut a thin strip of cardboard from the cardboard tube to make the eyes. Roll it and squash it.

FLYING BUG

1 Scrunch newspaper into a body shape. Use masking tape to get the shape you are happy with.

2 Make the legs out of pipe cleaners, using the same method as for the Hopping Bug.

Attach the legs to the body with masking tape.

3 Make the little wings out of plastic packaging or cardboard if you prefer. You need to bend the straight edge into a flap to allow you to glue the wing to the body.

Decorate the wing (this is easier to do before fixing onto the body).

flap to glue

4 Make two antennae out of paper clips or thin wire. Open them out and wind around a pencil, attaching with masking tape.

5 Use paper towel instead of newspaper for the paper-mache stage. Cover the bug's body. Once dry, you can paint your bug in flying colors and stick on the eyes!

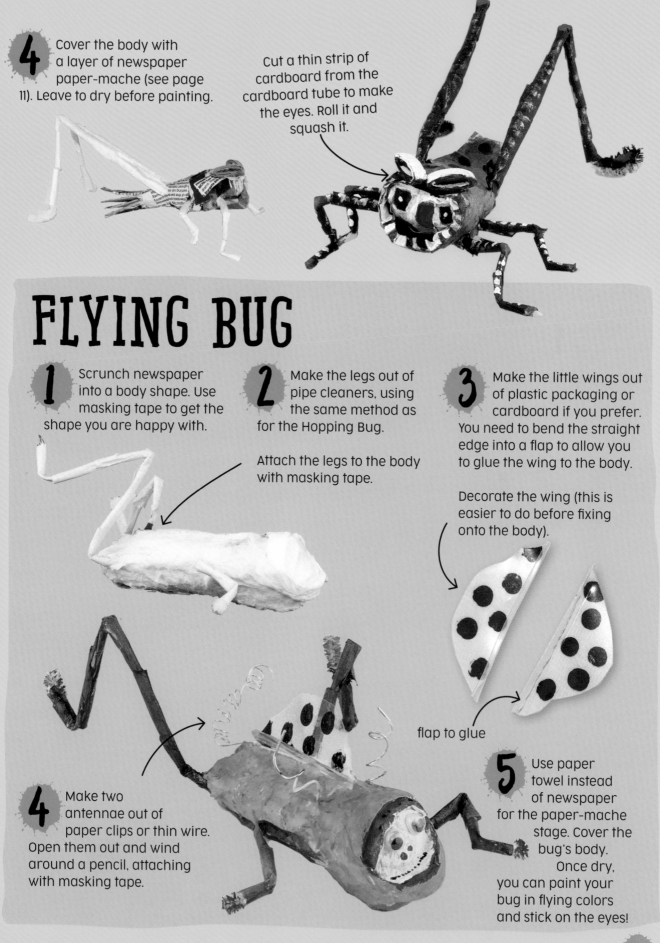

STICK INSECT

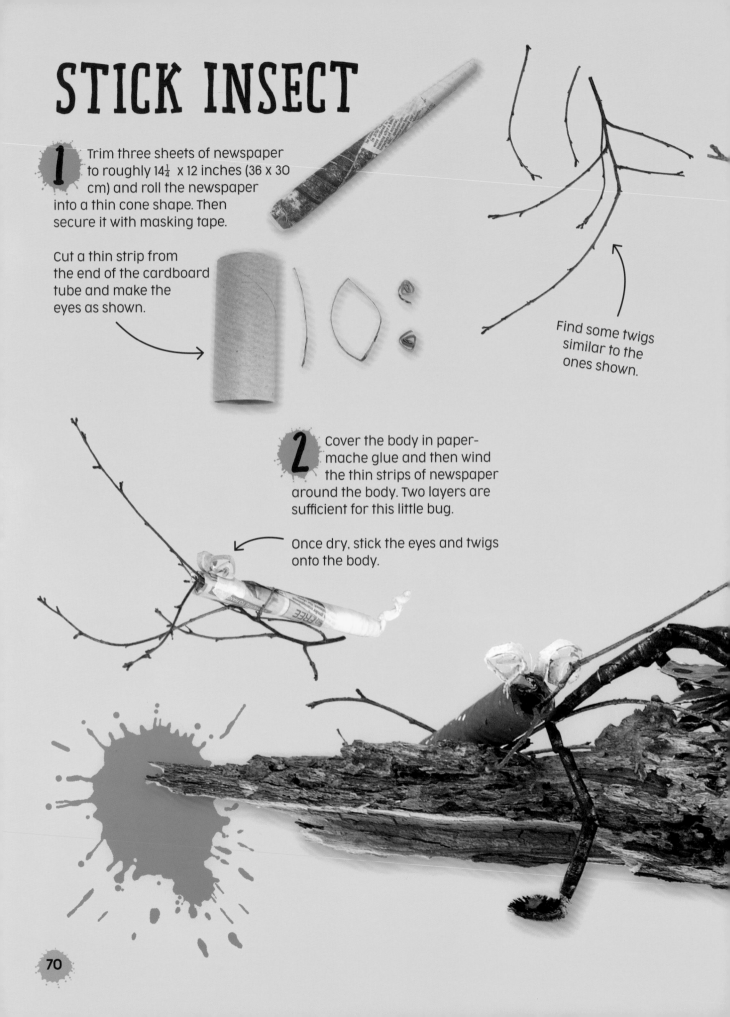

1 Trim three sheets of newspaper to roughly 14¼ x 12 inches (36 x 30 cm) and roll the newspaper into a thin cone shape. Then secure it with masking tape.

Cut a thin strip from the end of the cardboard tube and make the eyes as shown.

Find some twigs similar to the ones shown.

2 Cover the body in paper-mache glue and then wind the thin strips of newspaper around the body. Two layers are sufficient for this little bug.

Once dry, stick the eyes and twigs onto the body.

3 Paint the stick insect in your favorite bug color!

MUMMY IN THE CUPBOARD

FOR THE MUMMY

YOU WILL NEED

Pipe cleaners
Tissue
Masking tape
Newspaper
Paper-mache glue
(see page 11)
Torn cotton material
Paint
Plastic eyes (optional)
Cold coffee or tea
Stiff cardboard
Corrugated cardboard
Beads
Plain or watercolor paper

1 Make an elongated head shape using two pipe cleaners. Loop one on top of the other, leaving enough at the bottom to form the neck.

2 Use soft tissue to pad out the inside of the head, but put less tissue in at the bottom half to leave room for the mouth.

3 Wrap the head in masking tape, starting at the top. When you get to the mouth area, cut two strips of masking tape. Fold one edge in on itself then stick one on the top of the mouth area and one on the bottom of the mouth area. This will give the mummy an open-mouthed look.

4 For the body, use three sheets of newspaper and roll into a thin cone shape. Trim to about 5 inches (13 cm) in length and secure with masking tape.
The neck beneath the mummy's head should be pushed into the thin end of the body cone and secured in place with masking tape.

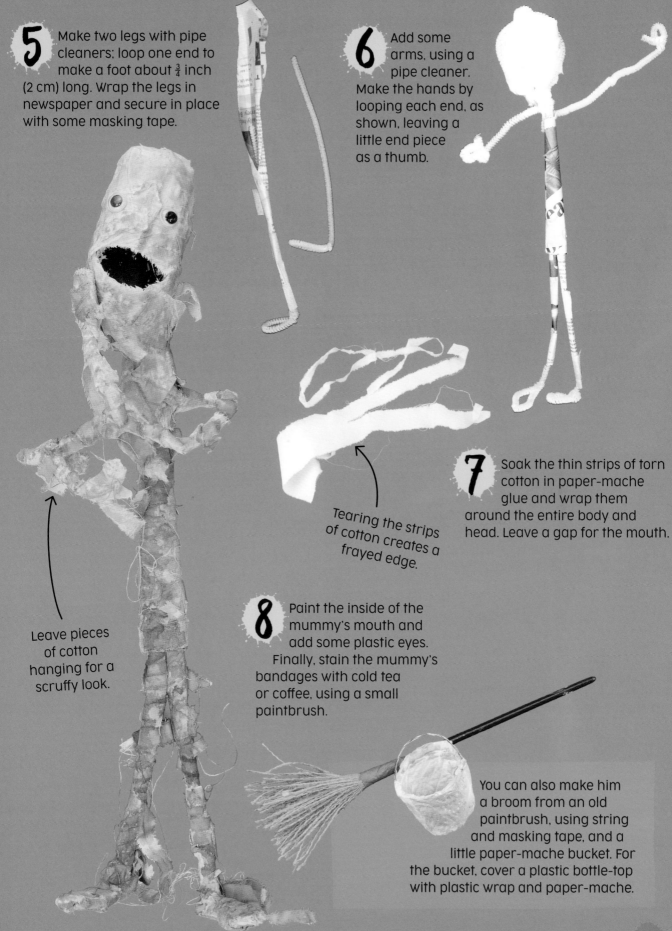

5 Make two legs with pipe cleaners; loop one end to make a foot about ¾ inch (2 cm) long. Wrap the legs in newspaper and secure in place with some masking tape.

6 Add some arms, using a pipe cleaner. Make the hands by looping each end, as shown, leaving a little end piece as a thumb.

7 Soak the thin strips of torn cotton in paper-mache glue and wrap them around the entire body and head. Leave a gap for the mouth.

Tearing the strips of cotton creates a frayed edge.

Leave pieces of cotton hanging for a scruffy look.

8 Paint the inside of the mummy's mouth and add some plastic eyes. Finally, stain the mummy's bandages with cold tea or coffee, using a small paintbrush.

You can also make him a broom from an old paintbrush, using string and masking tape, and a little paper-mache bucket. For the bucket, cover a plastic bottle-top with plastic wrap and paper-mache.

MUMMY'S CUPBOARD

Make your mummy a cupboard out of stiff cardboard—it can be any size you like.

1 Take one piece of stiff cardboard, bending it at both ends to make doors and allow it to stand up. To make the doors more realistic, add corrugated cardboard panels, glue on beads for handles and paint the doors with acrylic paint.

2 Measure the back panel and trim some plain paper to size (watercolor paper works well, but plain paper is fine, too). Glue the paper to the back panel and paint the background in a neutral color.

When dry, draw on two shelves as in the picture.

3 Draw a rack below and add some objects hanging from hooks. Add bottles and jars on the shelves. You can draw them or cut out pictures from a magazine.

Use a template to draw your jars.

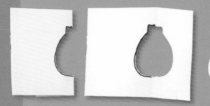

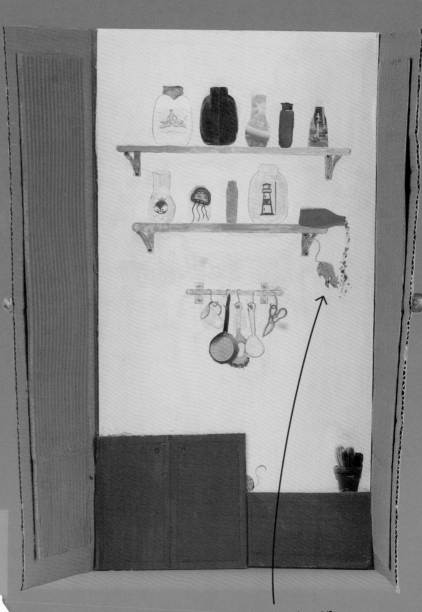

Add some mice or rats for fun.

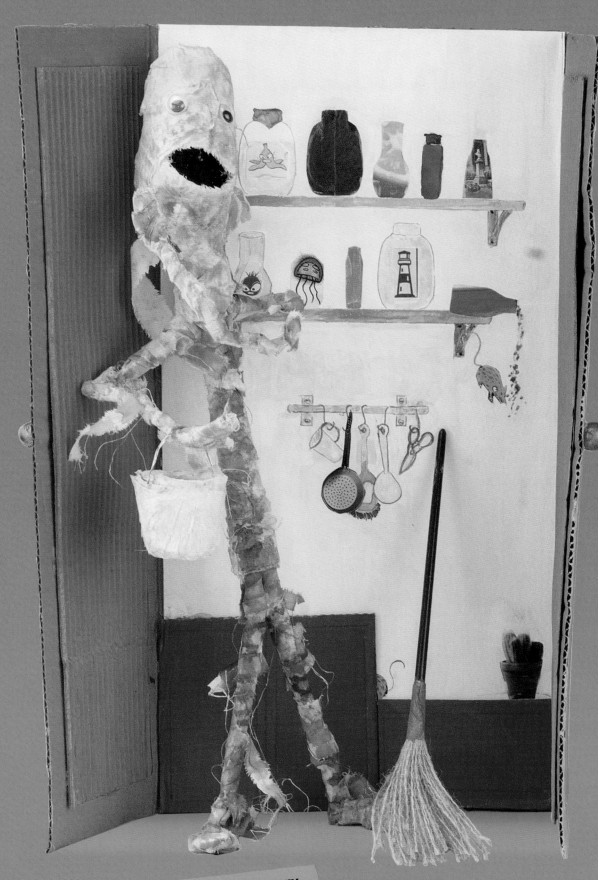

Your mummy will be very much at home here!

BASKET SKULL

Here is a great desk game to play at Halloween, or any time of the year. The skeleton's skull is the basketball!

YOU WILL NEED

For the skeleton:

Pipe cleaners

Cotton balls or scrunched-up tissues

Masking tape

String

Cereal box cardboard

For the base and basketball net:

Stiff cardboard

Long tube from pastic wrap or aluminum foil

Glue

Pipe cleaner

Vegetable net

Masking tape

String

Paper-mache glue and paper towels
(see page 11)

Paint

1 To strengthen your skeleton, double up your pipe cleaners by winding one around another. Make six of these and then...
- Use one for the legs.
- Use one for the arms.
- Use one or two for the ribs.
- Use one for the head.
- Use the last one doubled up for the hands.

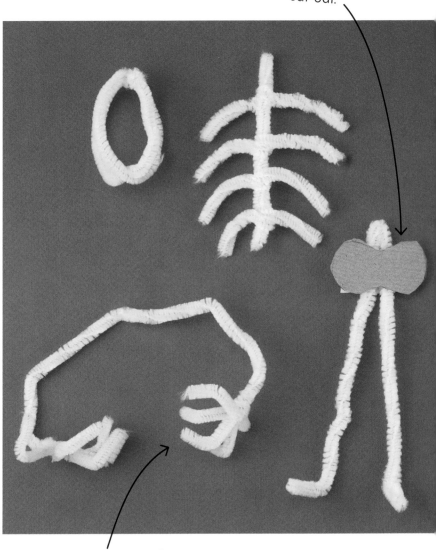

Here is the hip cut-out.

Make the body parts as shown (the head is two loops, one over the other).

2 Stuff the skull with cotton balls or tissue and glue on string for the hair.

Carefully wrap the skull in masking tape (cut the tape in half, and use smaller strips).

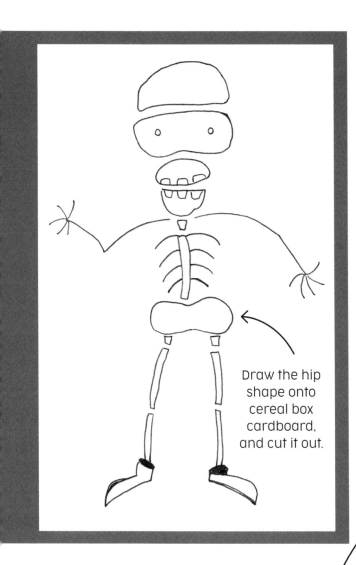

Draw the hip shape onto cereal box cardboard, and cut it out.

Make a base out of stiff cardboard. Glue the long cardboard tube to the base.

3 Tape the hips onto the legs with masking tape.

Attach the bottom of the ribs to the legs with masking tape.

Wind the arms around the top of the ribs.

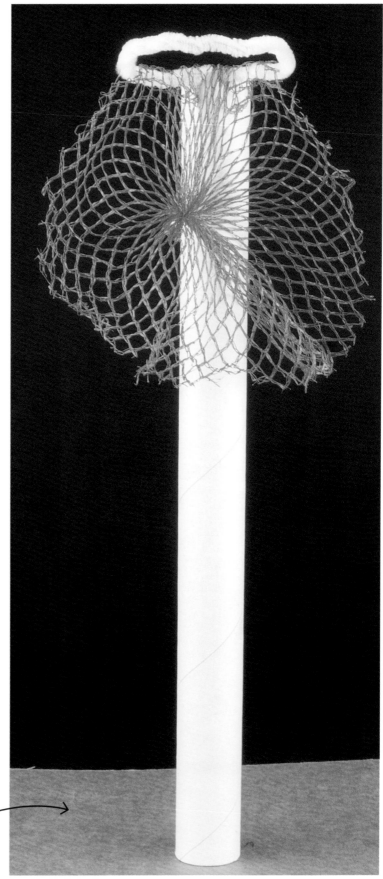

4 For the basketball net, make a backboard out of stiff cardboard. Measure and make two slits in the backboard so you can slot it onto the tube.

Make a basketball hoop with a pipe cleaner and attach with masking tape.

Add the netting to the hoop and fix by winding the string in and out of the hoop and net.

Cover the base with paper-mache for added strength before painting.

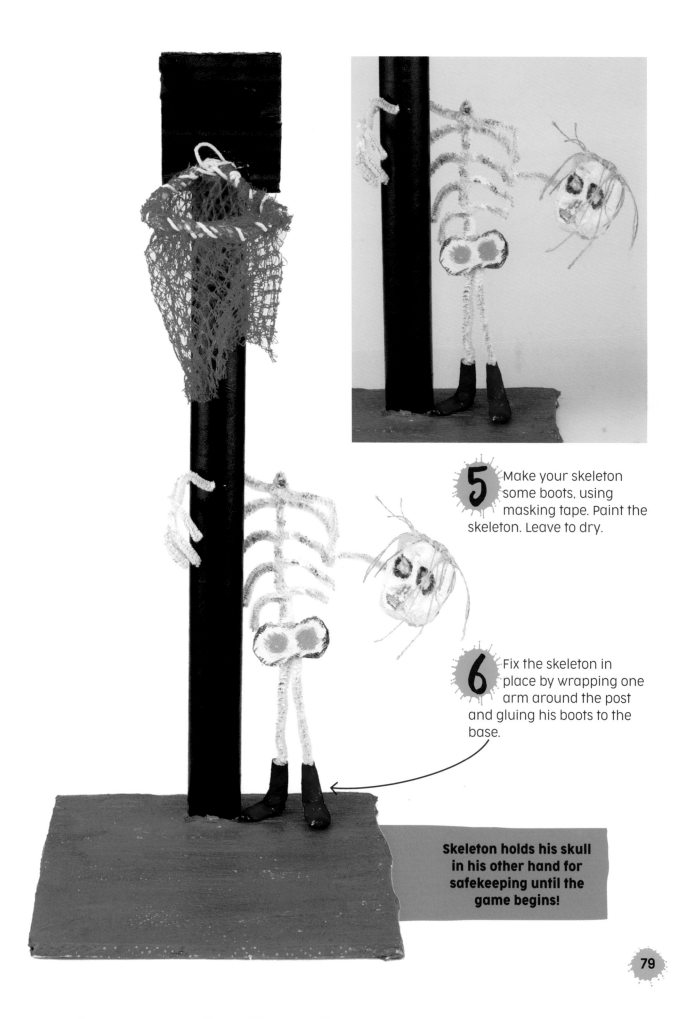

5 Make your skeleton some boots, using masking tape. Paint the skeleton. Leave to dry.

6 Fix the skeleton in place by wrapping one arm around the post and gluing his boots to the base.

Skeleton holds his skull in his other hand for safekeeping until the game begins!

SECRET CAT

Don't give up the secret to anyone when you make this secret cat!

YOU WILL NEED

Balloon

Plastic cap (from a baking soda tub or similar)

Newspaper and paper-mache glue (see page 11)

Cardboard

Corks x 4

Strong glue and school glue (PVA)

Cotton balls

Masking tape

Pipe cleaner

Paper-mache powder or tissue

1 Inflate the balloon and, on the underside, draw a circle using the plastic cap as a template. Cover the balloon with two good layers of paper-mache, leaving the circle uncovered. Leave to dry.

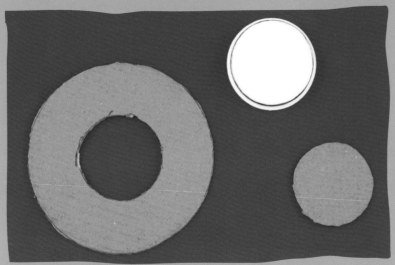

2 Draw around the plastic cap on some cardboard, then draw a bigger circle around it, wide enough for the corks to fit on. Cut out as shown.

3 Glue the corks to the cardboard ring. Make some feet out of cardboard and glue them to the bottom of each cork.

Line up the ring to the uncovered circle on the paper-mache balloon and glue securely.

4 For the head, make a ball shape with cotton balls and tape it to the body as shown: make ears out of cardboard and attach with masking tape.

5 For the tail, wind cotton balls around a long pipe cleaner and cover with masking tape. Attach to the paper-mache balloon with more tape.

6 Cover the head, body and tail with two more layers of paper-mache and leave to dry. Make some toes out of paper-mache powder (see page 10) or rolled-up tissue soaked in glue.

Pop the balloon inside the cat and remove.

7 Paint the cat with your favorite color. When dry, finish with a layer of school glue (PVA).

You can hide all of your treasures in the secret opening, under the cat's tummy!

BEASTLY BATS

Some blood-sucking bats are always a favorite around the house. These two will make great pets, or you can make more to create your own bat colony.

FLYING BAT

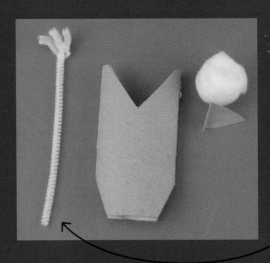

1 Flatten a cardboard tube and cut it into the shape shown here. Cut out some ears from the off-cuts.

Make two legs and feet out of pipe cleaners.

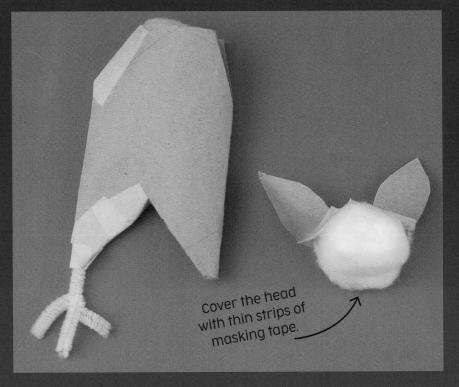

2 Use masking tape to fix the legs inside the body and fix the ears to a cotton ball to make the head. Stuff the body with more cotton balls and seal the ends with masking tape.

Cover the head with thin strips of masking tape.

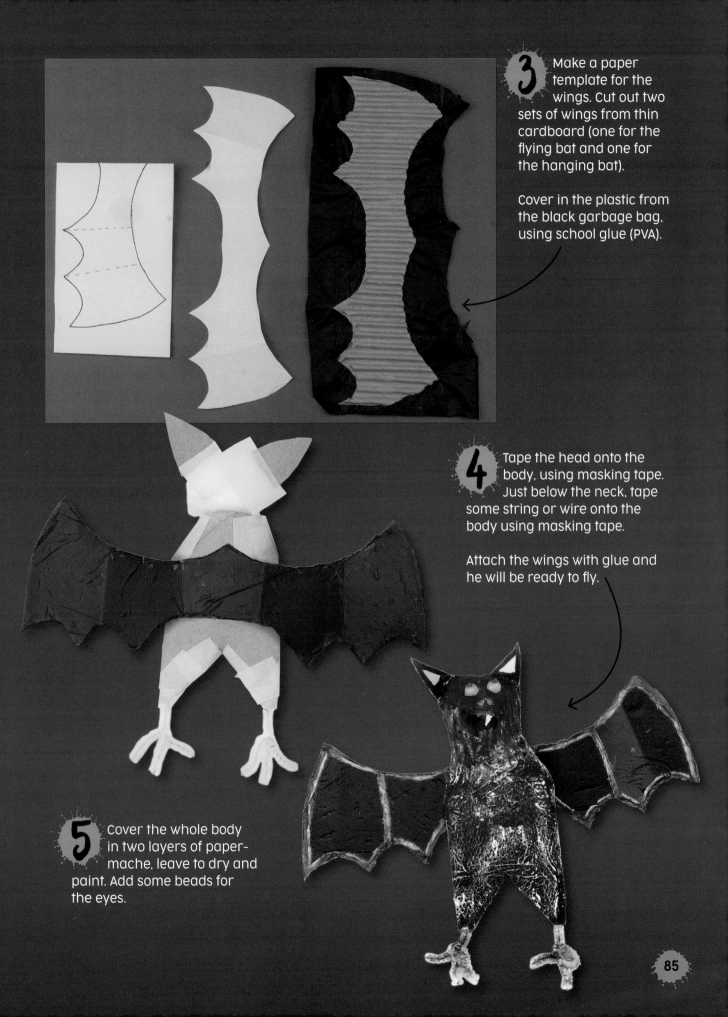

3 Make a paper template for the wings. Cut out two sets of wings from thin cardboard (one for the flying bat and one for the hanging bat).

Cover in the plastic from the black garbage bag, using school glue (PVA).

4 Tape the head onto the body, using masking tape. Just below the neck, tape some string or wire onto the body using masking tape.

Attach the wings with glue and he will be ready to fly.

5 Cover the whole body in two layers of paper-mache, leave to dry and paint. Add some beads for the eyes.

HANGING BAT

6 Flatten a cardboard tube but, this time, draw a line as shown. Then cut along the line to make a thinner body.

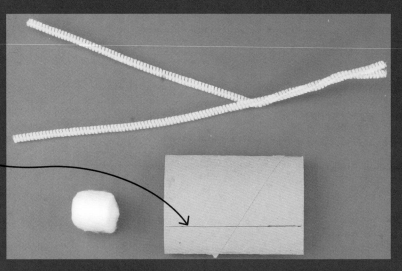

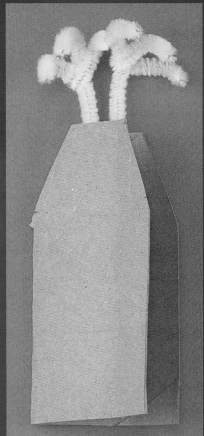

7 Cut out the shape shown and make some legs and feet as before. Fix them inside the body with masking tape.
Tape and seal the open edge to the side and at the feet end.

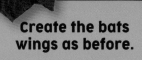

Create the bats wings as before.

8 Pad out the body with cotton balls as before. Make a head as before, cover in masking tape and attach to the body. Cover with paper-mache and leave to dry.

9 Paint your hanging bat, add beads for the eyes and the wings, and fold the wings as shown.

Make a cool colony
of bats to hang out
with you.

PAINTBRUSH PALS

This is really fun to do, and the older and scruffier the paintbrushes, the better!

YOU WILL NEED

Paintbrushes x 2
Masking tape
Pipe cleaners x 2
String
Nuts, washers, and beads
Cardboard
Material (some old denim would be perfect)
Glue
Small brackets
Wooden clothes pins x 4
Paint

1 You may not have all of the things used here, but you will be able to find your own odds and ends that will do the job!

2 Add masking tape to the brush heads as shown to give them different hairstyles. Try taping the bristles down to encourage them to stand out and create a fringe.

Wind string around the pipe cleaner.

Change the hairstyle.

3 Use the pipe cleaners to make the two sets of arms. Thread on some nuts and washers or beads. Make a little hand at both ends to stop them falling off.

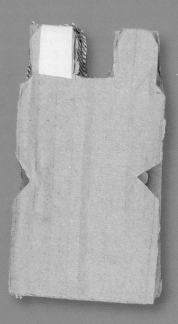

4 Cut out the shape of the work apron twice (make sure it is large enough to cover the handle of the brush).

Wind the arms around the paintbrush before step 6.

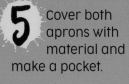

5 Cover both aprons with material and make a pocket.

6 Glue the front and back apron onto one of the paintbrushes.

Add the little brackets for the feet.

7 Make some shoulder tabs. The tabs glue onto the front and back of the apron.

Add nuts for the features or just paint the face.

Add something to the pocket (this small screwdriver came out of a party cracker).

Paint the hair and body different colors.

8 Glue the clothes pins together in pairs and glue them to the front and back of the other paintbrush handle.

Wrap the arms around as shown.

Glue on the eyes, nose, and mouth. Then, start painting!